ANDREW LLOYD WEBBER™

CONTENTS

Andrew Lloyd Webber™ is a trademark owned by Andrew Lloyd Webber.

— PIANO LEVEL —
LATE INTERMEDIATE/EARLY ADVANCED

ISBN 978-0-634-05660-4

T0055387

HAL•LEONARD®
CORPORATION
7777 W. BLUEMOUND RD. P.O. BOX 13819 MILWAUKEE, WI 53213

For all works contained herein:
Unauthorized copying, arranging, adapting, recording or public performance is an infringement of copyright.
Infringers are liable under the law.

The musical works contained in this edition may not be publicly performed in a dramatic form or context
except under license from The Really Useful Group Limited, 22 Tower Street, London WC2H 9NS

Visit Hal Leonard Online at
www.halleonard.com

ALL I ASK OF YOU
from THE PHANTOM OF THE OPERA

Music by ANDREW LLOYD WEBBER
Lyrics by CHARLES HART
Additional Lyrics by RICHARD STILGOE
Arranged by Phillip Keveren

Flowing, deeply expressive

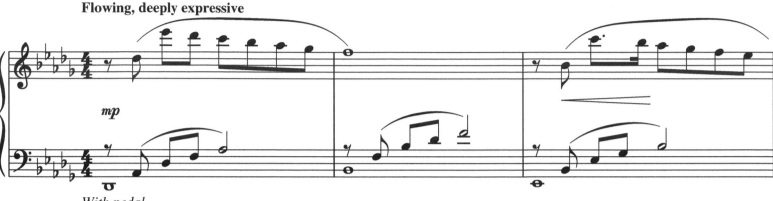

© Copyright 1986 The Really Useful Group Ltd.
This arrangement © Copyright 2000 The Really Useful Group Ltd.
All Rights for the United States and Canada Administered by Universal - PolyGram International Publishing, Inc.
International Copyright Secured   All Rights Reserved

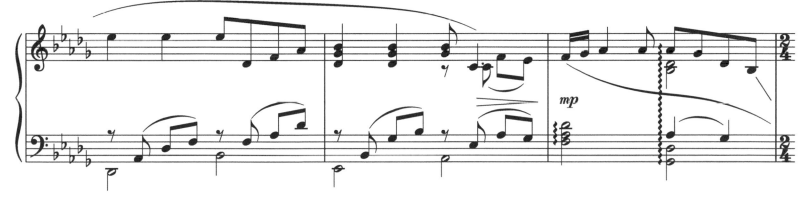

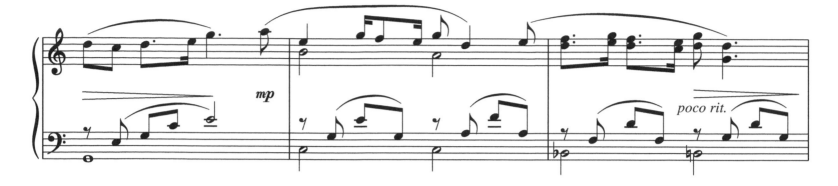

With drama

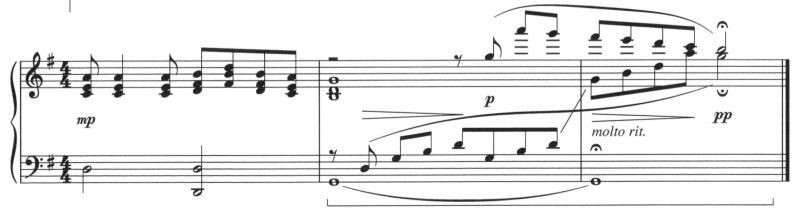

ANY DREAM WILL DO

from JOSEPH AND THE AMAZING TECHNICOLOR® DREAMCOAT

Music by ANDREW LLOYD WEBBER
Lyrics by TIM RICE
Arranged by Phillip Keveren

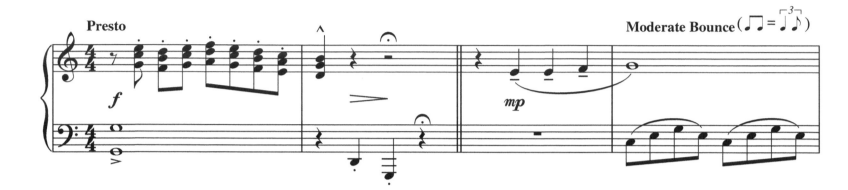

© Copyright 1969 The Really Useful Group Ltd.
Copyright Renewed
This arrangement © Copyright 2003 The Really Useful Group Ltd.
All Rights for North America Controlled by Williamson Music Co.
International Copyright Secured   All Rights Reserved

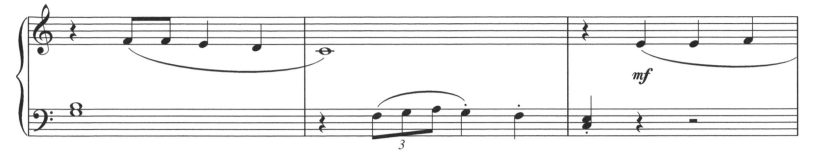

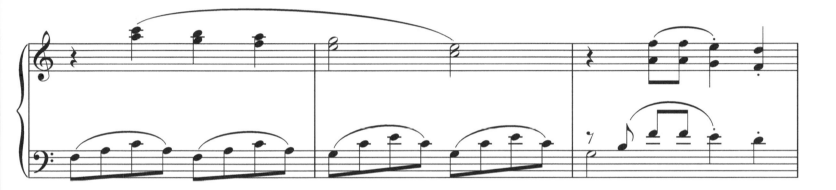

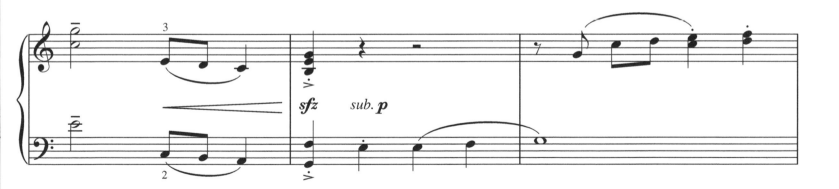

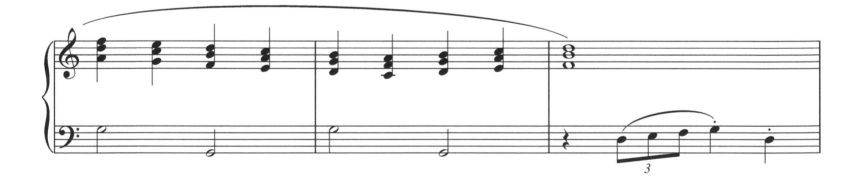

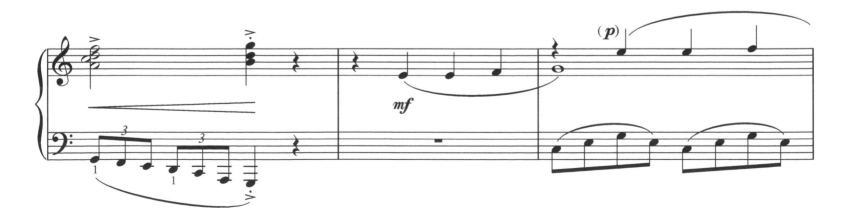

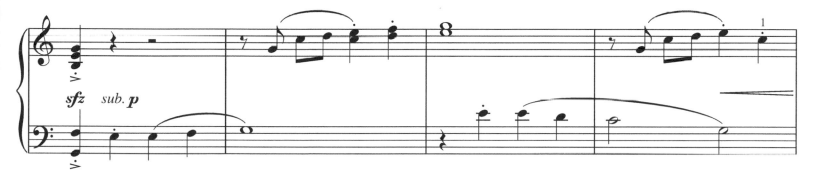

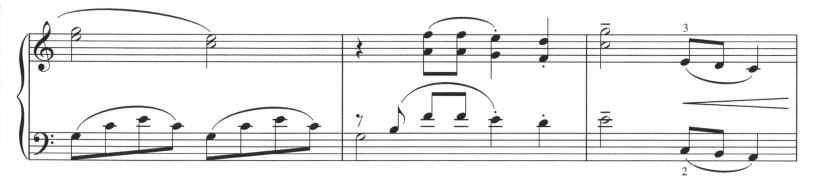

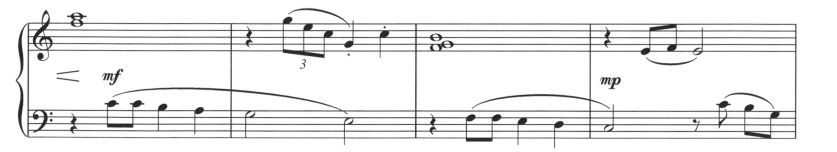

AS IF WE NEVER SAID GOODBYE

from SUNSET BOULEVARD

Music by ANDREW LLOYD WEBBER
Lyrics by DON BLACK and CHRISTOPHER HAMPTON,
with contributions by AMY POWERS
Arranged by Phillip Keveren

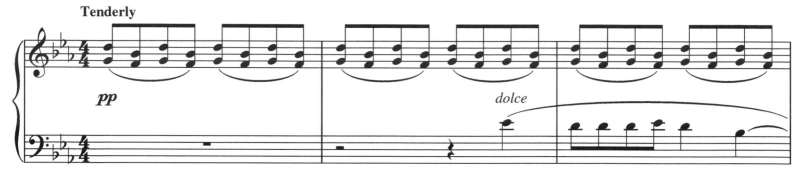

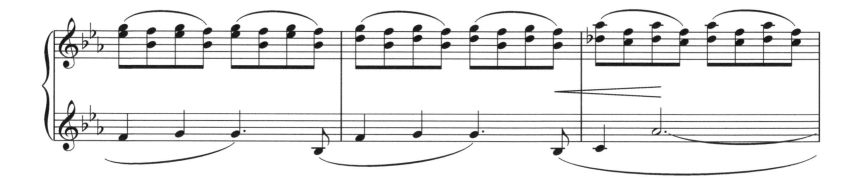

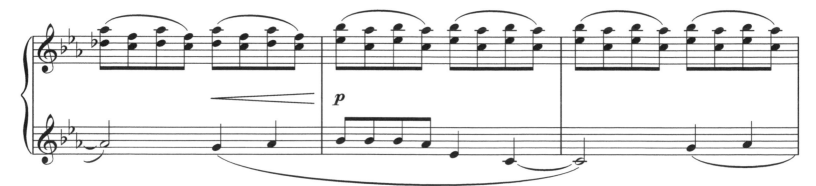

© Copyright 1993 The Really Useful Group Ltd.
This arrangement © Copyright 2003 The Really Useful Group Ltd.
All Rights for the United States Controlled by Famous Music Corporation
International Copyright Secured   All Rights Reserved

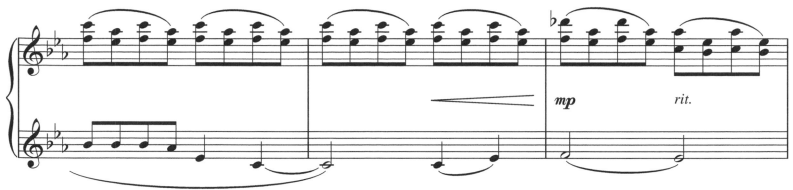

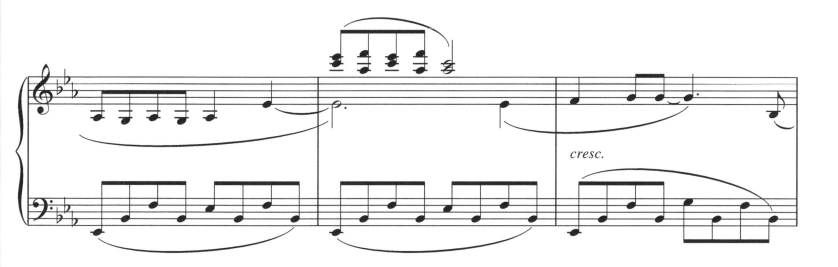

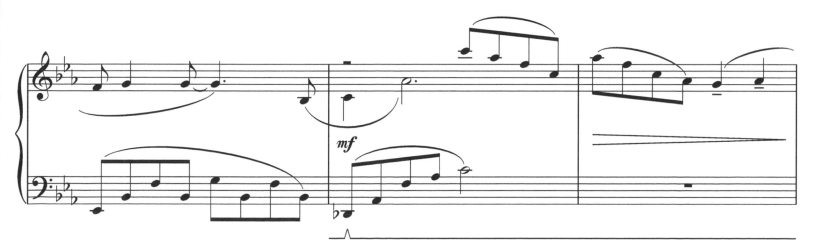

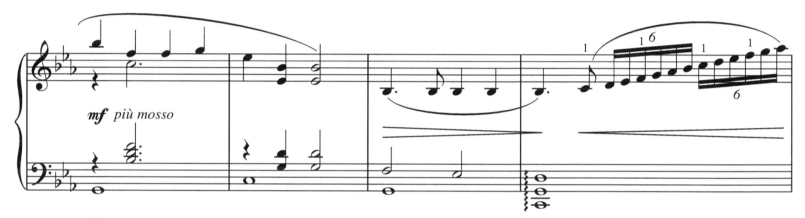

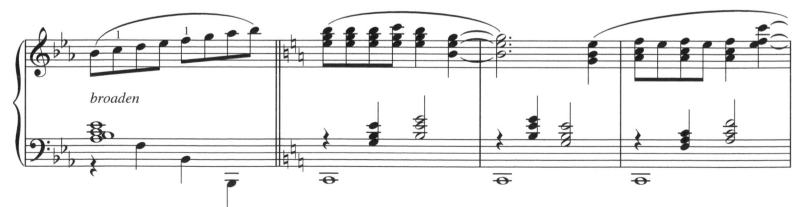

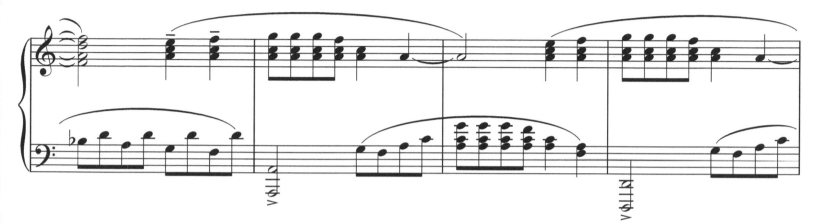

CLOSE EVERY DOOR

from JOSEPH AND THE AMAZING TECHNICOLOR® DREAMCOAT

Music by ANDREW LLOYD WEBBER
Lyrics by TIM RICE
Arranged by Phillip Keveren

Slowly, expressively

© Copyright 1969 The Really Useful Group Ltd.
Copyright Renewed
This arrangement © Copyright 2003 The Really Useful Group Ltd.
All Rights for North America Controlled by Williamson Music Co.
International Copyright Secured   All Rights Reserved

ername

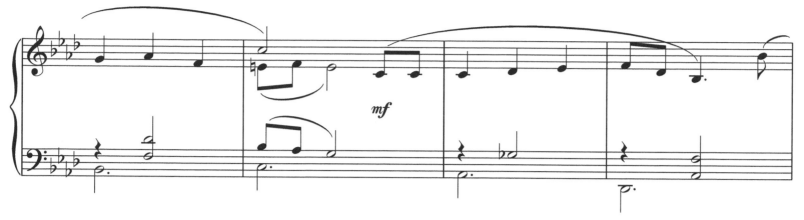

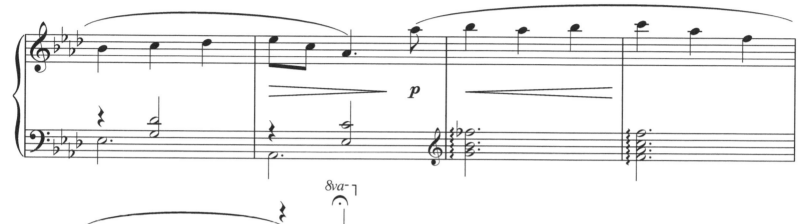

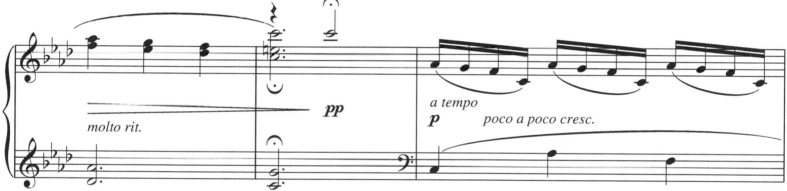

Maestoso

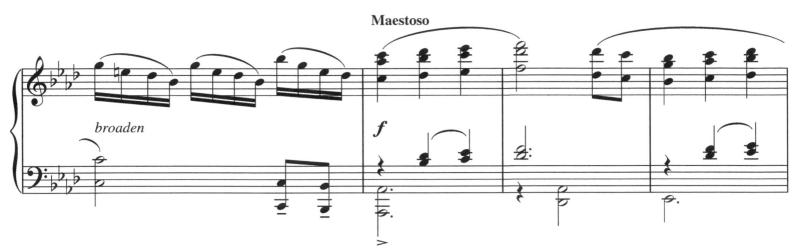

broaden

f

dim.

Tempo 1

pp

cresc.

mf

8va - - - - - - - - - - - - - -

f

pp

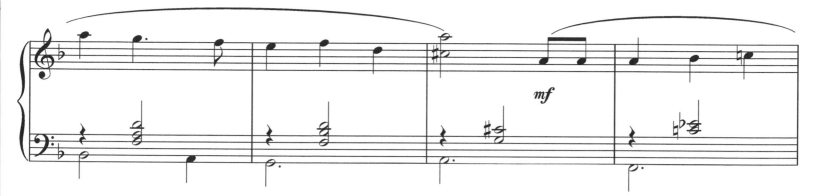

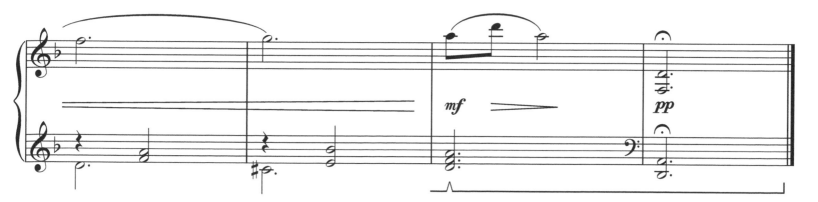

DON'T CRY FOR ME ARGENTINA

from EVITA

Words by TIM RICE
Music by ANDREW LLOYD WEBBER
Arranged by Phillip Keveren

Gently flowing

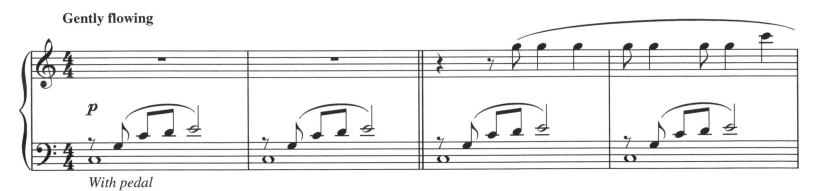

With pedal

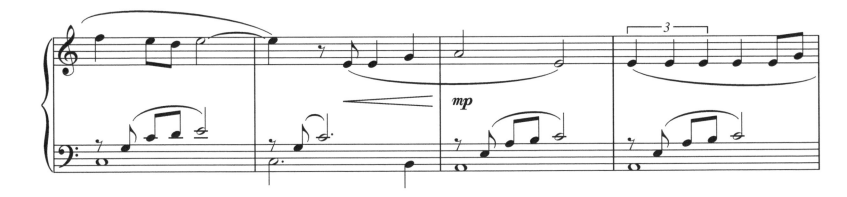

© 1976, 1977 EVITA MUSIC LTD.
This arrangement © 2003 EVITA MUSIC LTD.
All Rights for the U.S. and Canada Controlled and Administered by UNIVERSAL - ON BACKSTREET MUSIC, INC.
All Rights Reserved   Used by Permission

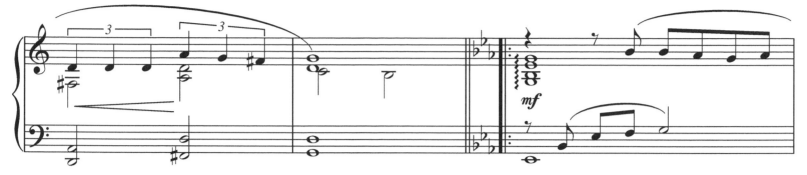

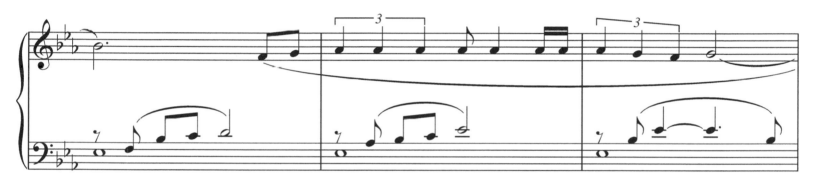

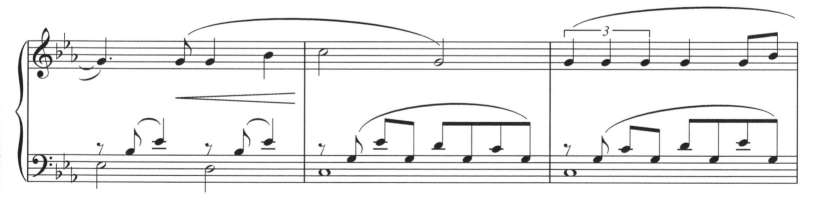

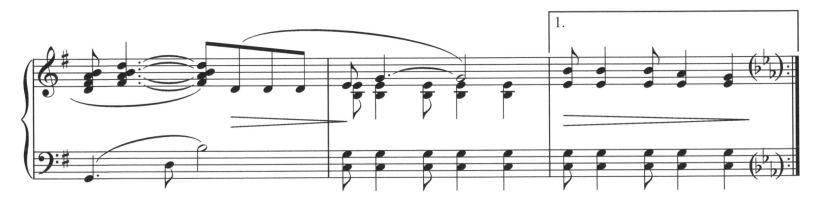

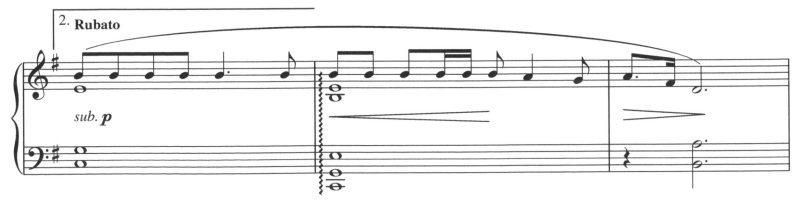

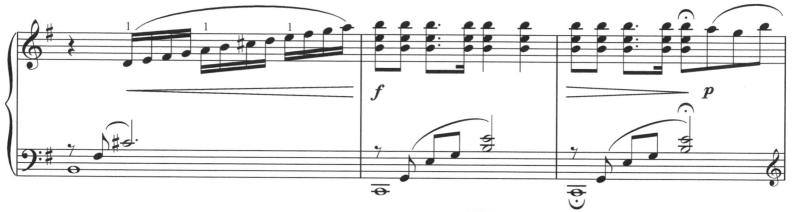

With grandeur

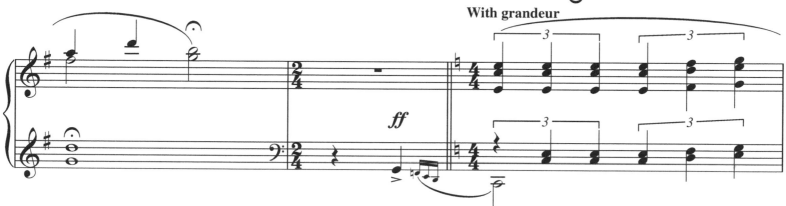

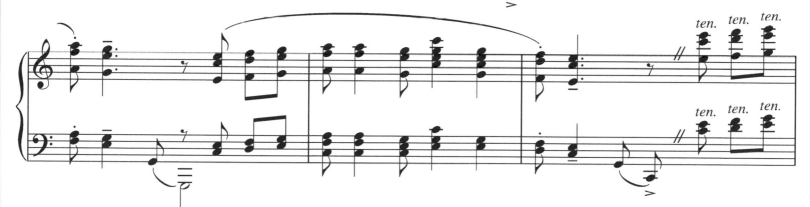

EVERYTHING'S ALRIGHT

from JESUS CHRIST SUPERSTAR

Words by TIM RICE
Music by ANDREW LLOYD WEBBER
Arranged by Phillip Keveren

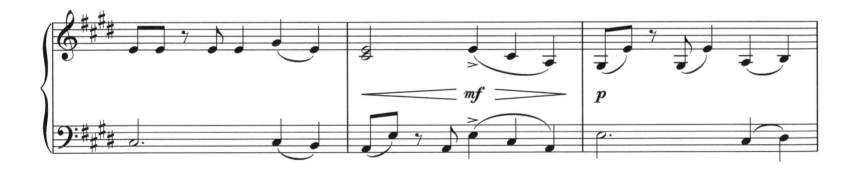

© 1970, 1971 LEEDS MUSIC LTD.
Copyrights Renewed
This arrangement © 2003 LEEDS MUSIC LTD.
All Rights for the U.S. and Canada Controlled and Administered by UNIVERSAL - MCA MUSIC PUBLISHING, A Division of UNIVERSAL STUDIOS, INC.
All Rights Reserved   Used by Permission

To Coda

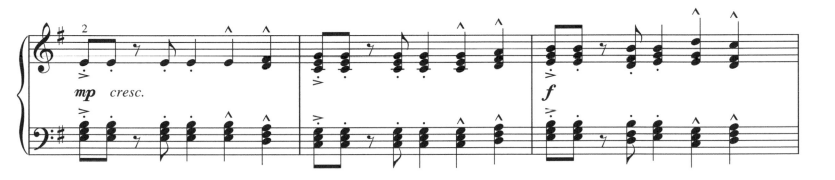

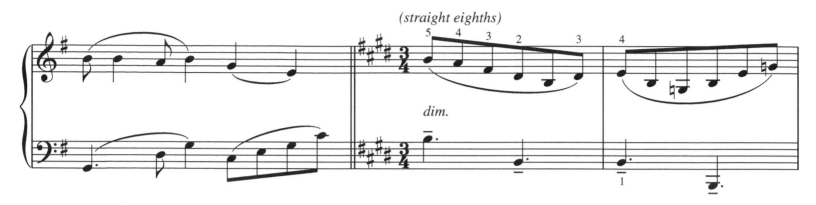

D.S. al Coda

CODA

MEMORY
from CATS

Music by ANDREW LLOYD WEBBER
Text by TREVOR NUNN after T.S. ELIOT
Arranged by Phillip Keveren

Moderately slow, expressively

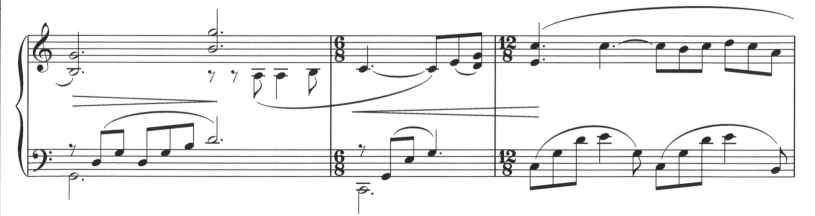

Music Copyright © 1981 The Really Useful Group Ltd.
Text Copyright © 1981 Trevor Nunn and Set Copyrights Ltd.
This arrangement Copyright © 2003 The Really Useful Group Ltd.
All Rights for The Really Useful Group Ltd. for the United States and Canada Administered by Universal - Songs Of PolyGram International, Inc.
All Rights in the text Controlled by Faber and Faber Ltd. and Administered for the United States and Canada by R&H Music Co.
International Copyright Secured   All Rights Reserved

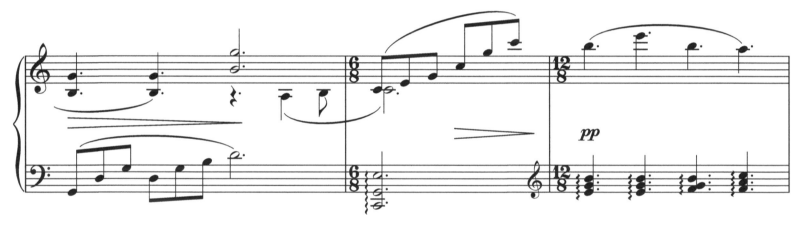

cresc. *f* *rit. e dim.* *mp* *a tempo*

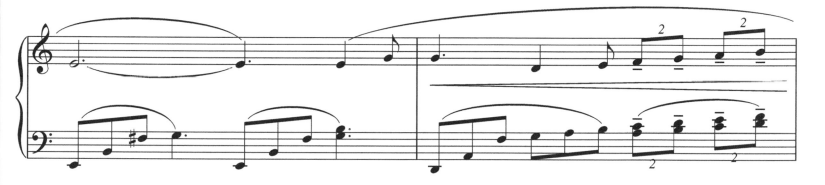

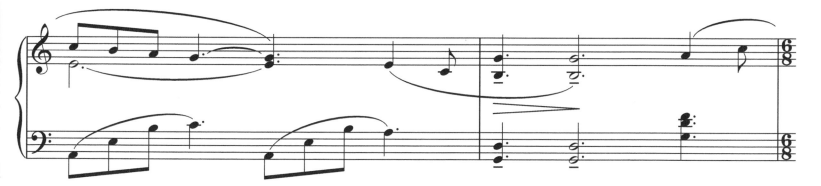

Maestoso

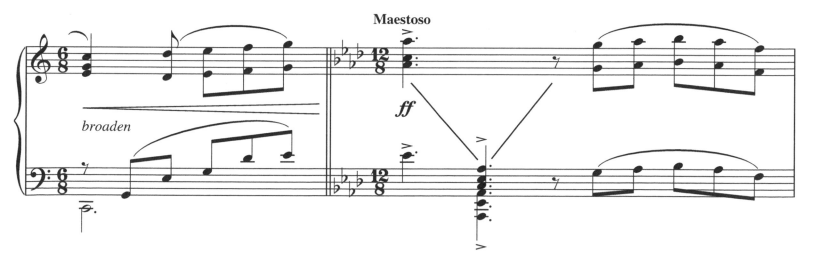

broaden *ff*

Più mosso

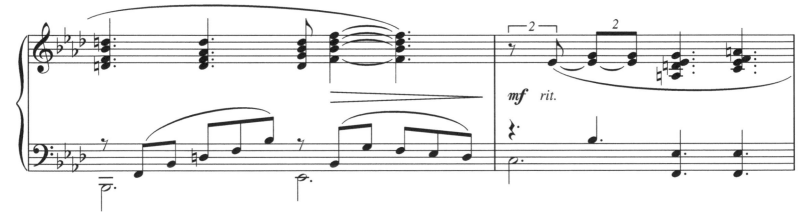

Soaring

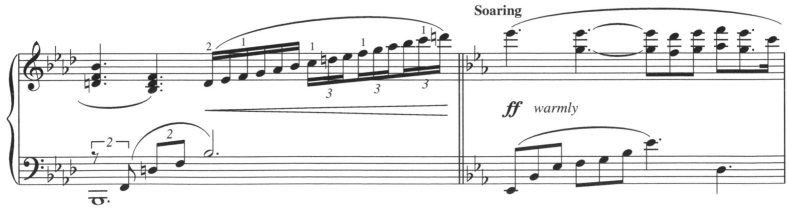

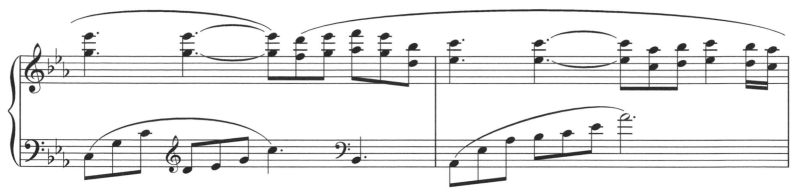

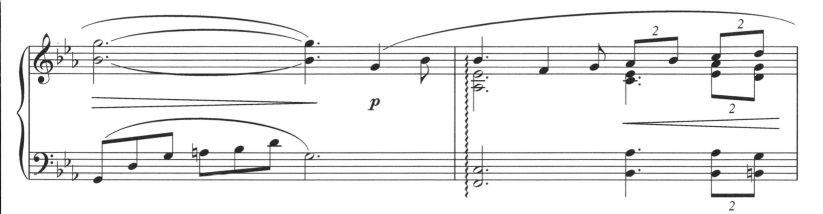

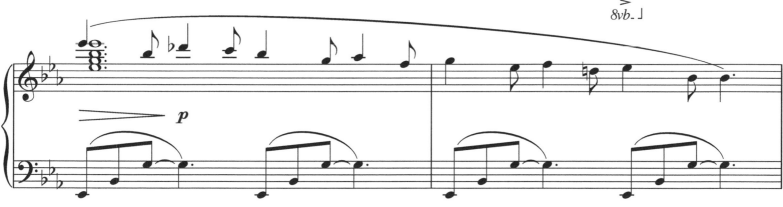

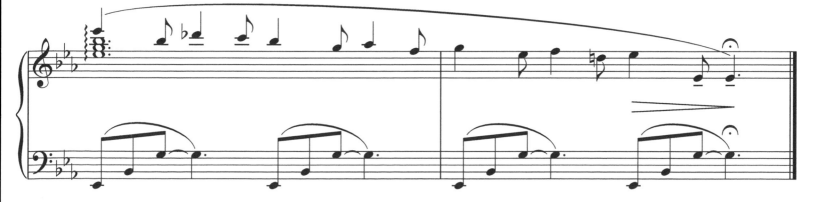

I AM THE STARLIGHT

from STARLIGHT EXPRESS

Music by ANDREW LLOYD WEBBER
Lyrics by RICHARD STILGOE
Arranged by Phillip Keveren

Flowing

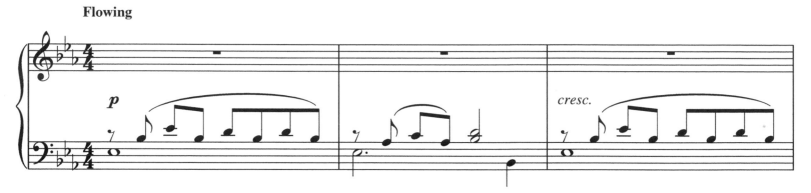

© Copyright 1984 The Really Useful Group Ltd.
This arrangement © Copyright 2003 The Really Useful Group Ltd.
All Rights for the United States and Canada Administered by Universal - PolyGram International Publishing, Inc.
International Copyright Secured   All Rights Reserved

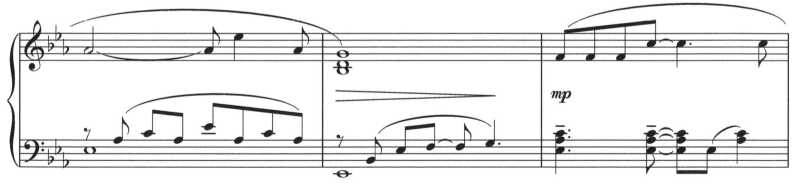

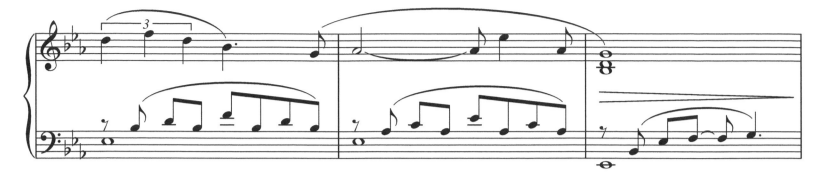

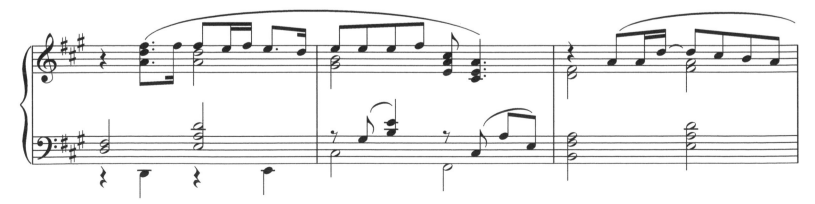

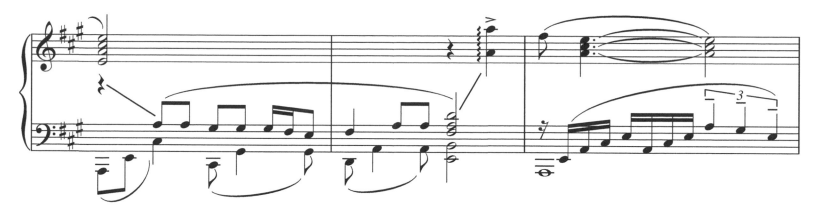

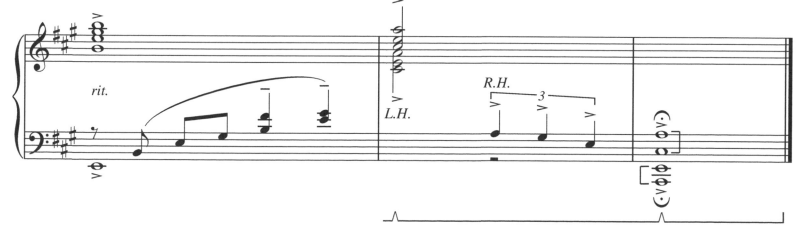

THE MUSIC OF THE NIGHT
from THE PHANTOM OF THE OPERA

Music by ANDREW LLOYD WEBBER
Lyrics by CHARLES HART
Additional Lyrics by RICHARD STILGOE
Arranged by Phillip Keveren

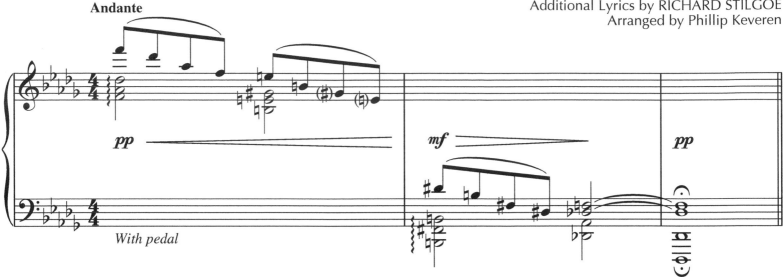

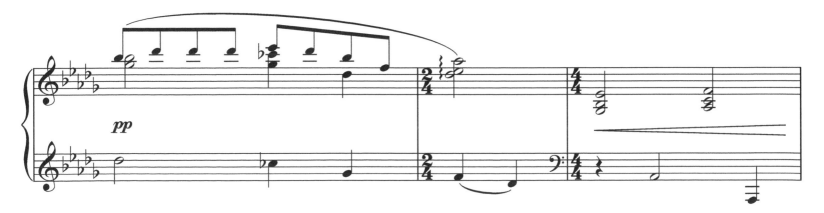

© Copyright 1986 The Really Useful Group Ltd.
This arrangement © Copyright 2003 The Really Useful Group Ltd.
All Rights for the United States and Canada Administered by Universal - PolyGram International Publishing, Inc.
International Copyright Secured   All Rights Reserved

36

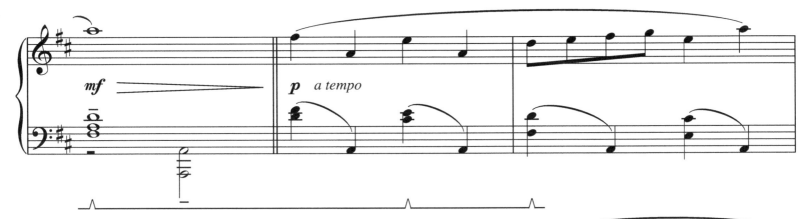

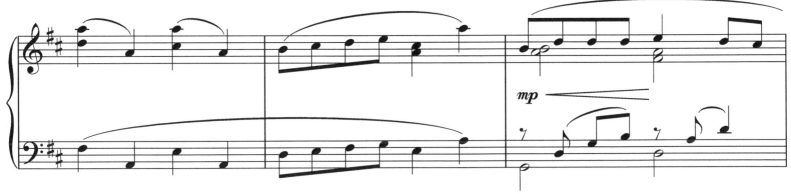

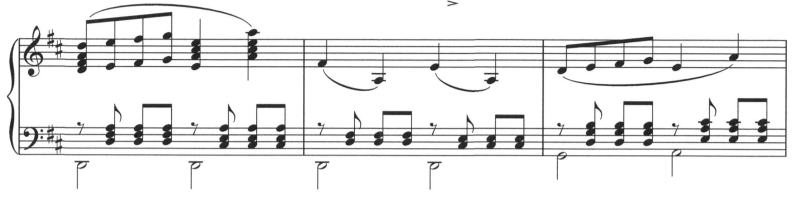
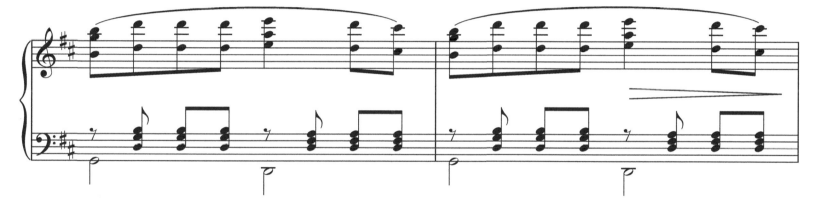

NO MATTER WHAT

from WHISTLE DOWN THE WIND

Music by ANDREW LLOYD WEBBER
Lyrics by JIM STEINMAN
Arranged by Phillip Keveren

Flowing, but unhurried

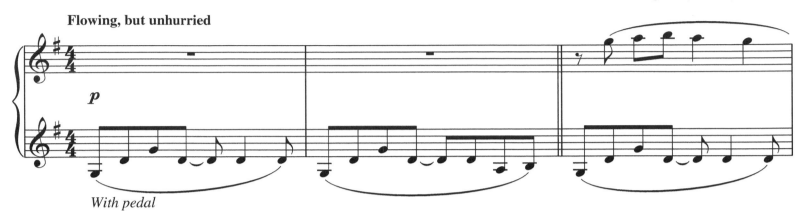

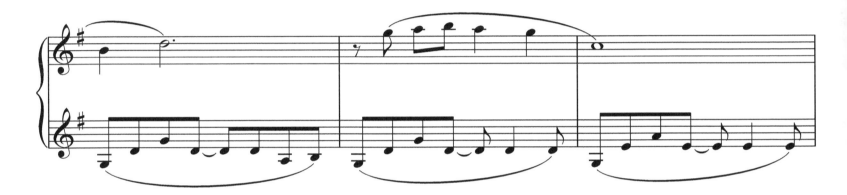

© Copyright 1996, 1998 The Really Useful Group Ltd., Universal - Songs Of PolyGram International, Inc. and Lost Boys Music
This arrangement © Copyright 2003 The Really Useful Group Ltd., Universal - Songs Of PolyGram International, Inc. and Lost Boys Music
All Rights for The Really Useful Group Ltd. in the United States and Canada Administered by Universal - PolyGram International Publishing, Inc.
International Copyright Secured   All Rights Reserved

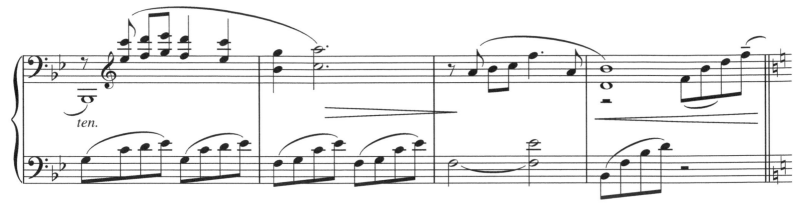

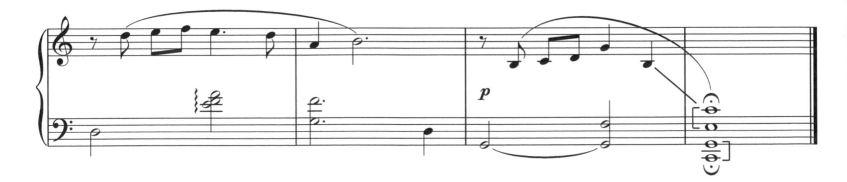

OUR KIND OF LOVE
from THE BEAUTIFUL GAME

Music by ANDREW LLOYD WEBBER
Lyrics by BEN ELTON
Arranged by Phillip Keveren

Slowly and tenderly

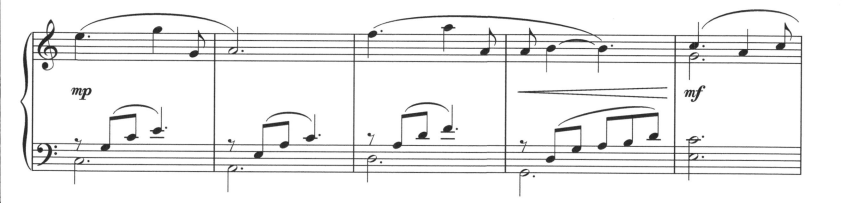

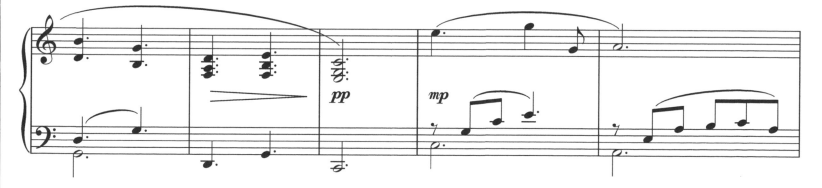

© Copyright 2000 The Really Useful Group Ltd.
This arrangement © Copyright 2003 The Really Useful Group Ltd.
International Copyright Secured   All Rights Reserved

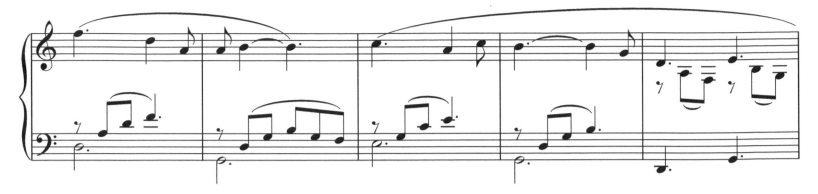

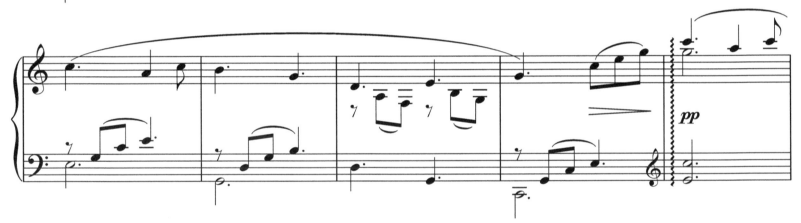

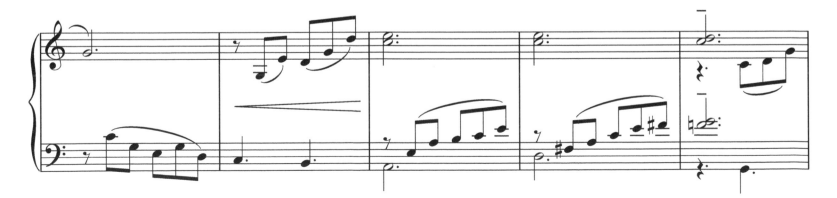

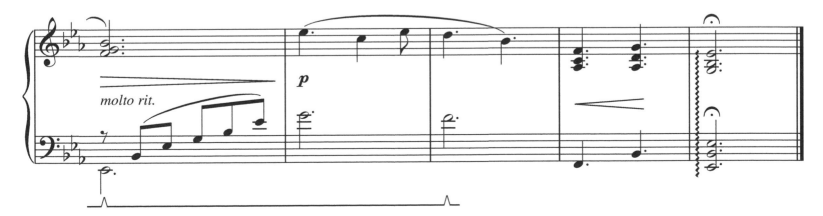

OLD DEUTERONOMY
from CATS

Music by ANDREW LLOYD WEBBER
Text by T.S. ELIOT
Arranged by Phillip Keveren

Slowly, quasi rubato, with drama

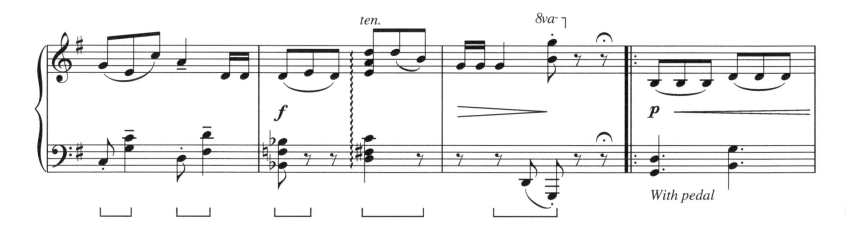

Music Copyright © 1980 The Really Useful Group Ltd.
Text Copyright © 1939 T.S. Eliot; this edition of the text © 1980 Set Copyrights Ltd.
This arrangement Copyright © 2003 The Really Useful Group Ltd.
All Rights for The Really Useful Group Ltd. for the United States and Canada Administered by Universal - Songs Of PolyGram International, Inc.
All Rights in the text Controlled by Faber and Faber Ltd. and Administered for the United States and Canada by R&H Music Co.
International Copyright Secured All Rights Reserved

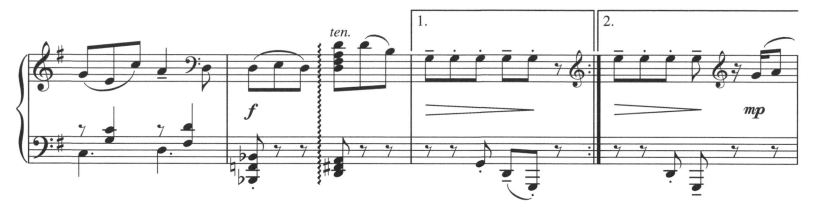

THE PHANTOM OF THE OPERA

from THE PHANTOM OF THE OPERA

Music by ANDREW LLOYD WEBBER
Lyrics by CHARLES HART
Additional Lyrics by RICHARD STILGOE and MIKE BATT
Arranged by Phillip Keveren

Maestoso

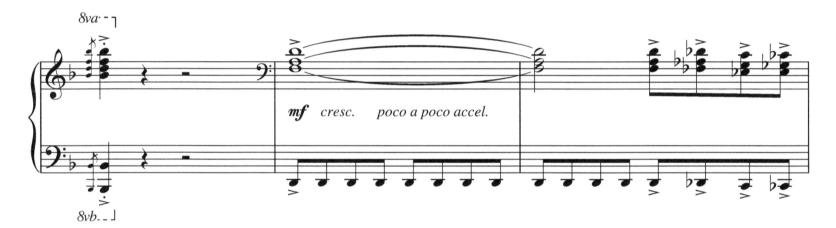

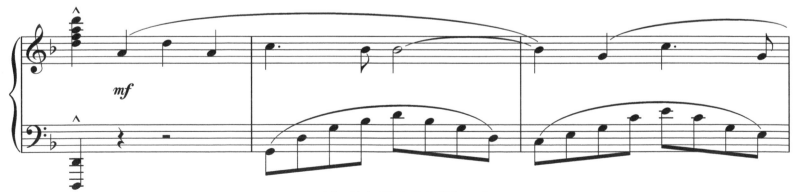

© Copyright 1986 The Really Useful Group Ltd.
This arrangement © Copyright 2003 The Really Useful Group Ltd.
All Rights for the United States and Canada Administered by Universal - PolyGram International Publishing, Inc.
International Copyright Secured   All Rights Reserved

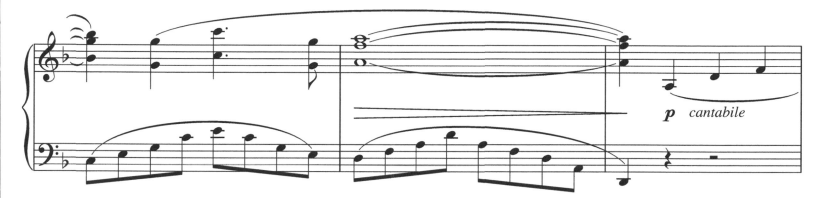

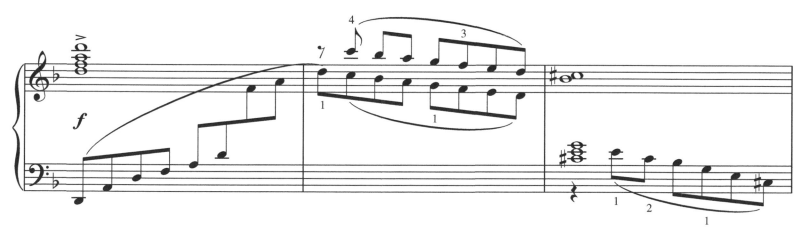

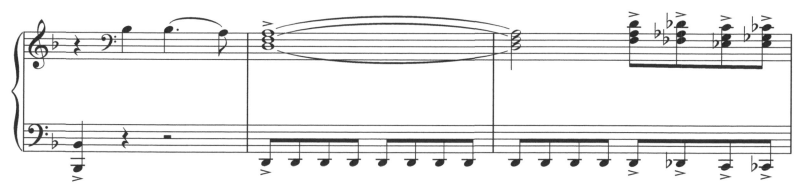

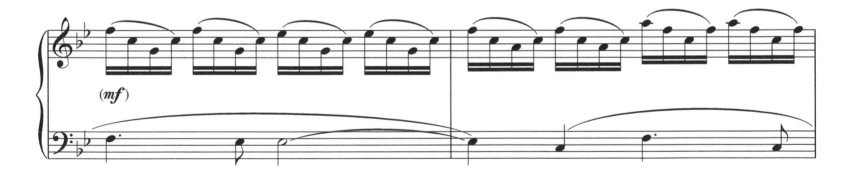

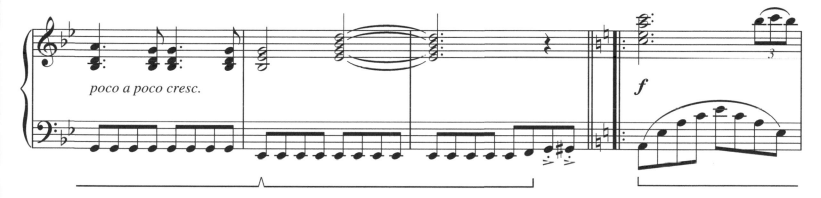

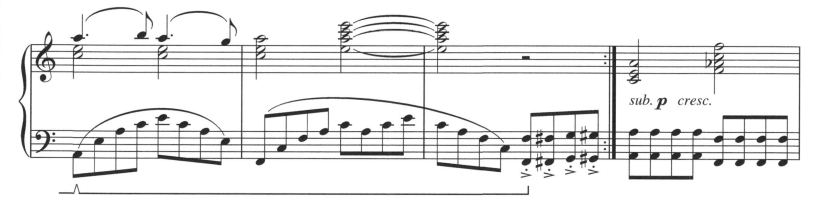

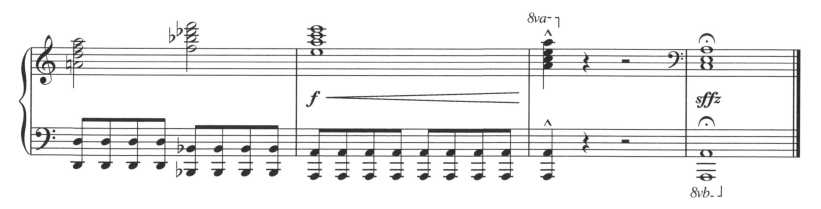

PIE JESU
from REQUIEM

By ANDREW LLOYD WEBBER
Arranged by Phillip Keveren

Andante

© Copyright 1985 The Really Useful Group Ltd.
This arrangement © Copyright 2003 The Really Useful Group Ltd.
All Rights for the United States and Canada Administered by Universal - PolyGram International Publishing, Inc.
International Copyright Secured   All Rights Reserved

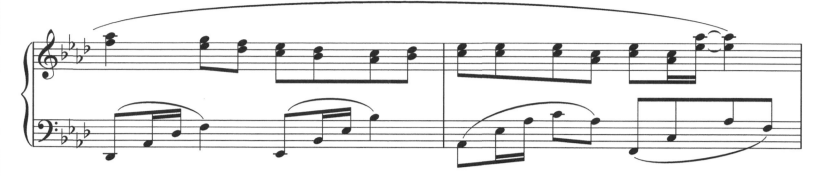

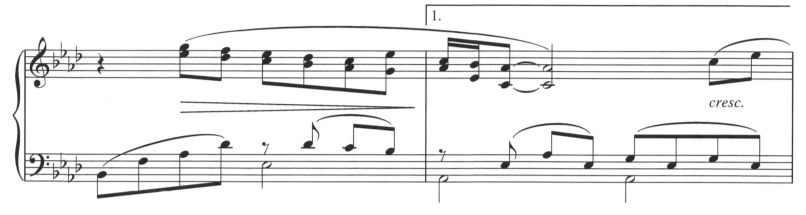

TELL ME ON A SUNDAY
from SONG AND DANCE

Music by ANDREW LLOYD WEBBER
Lyrics by DON BLACK
Arranged by Phillip Keveren

Animated

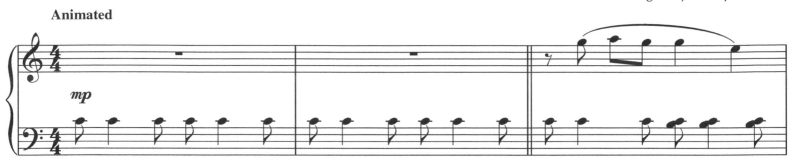

With pedal

© Copyright 1979 The Really Useful Group Ltd. and Dick James Music Ltd.
This arrangement © Copyright 2003 The Really Useful Group Ltd. and Dick James Music Ltd.
All Rights for the United States and Canada Administered by Universal - PolyGram International Publishing, Inc. and Universal - Songs Of PolyGram International, Inc.
International Copyright Secured   All Rights Reserved

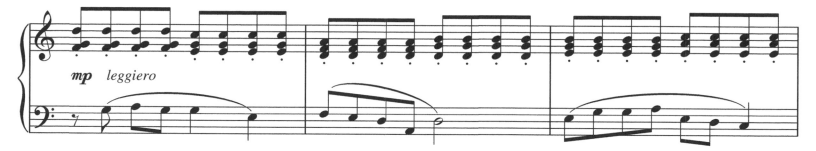

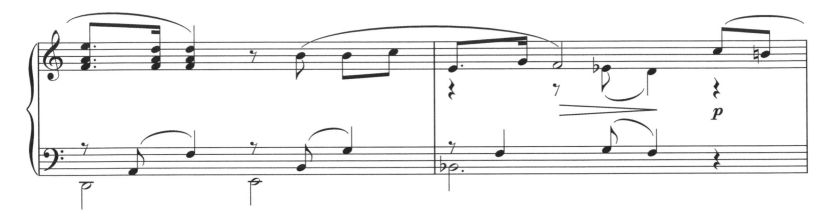

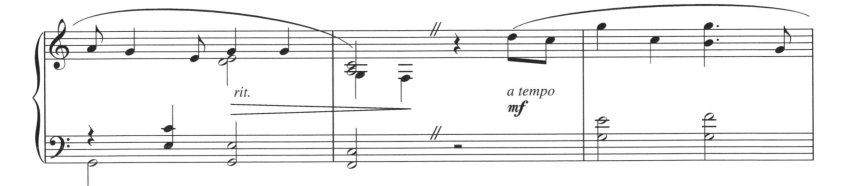

WHISTLE DOWN THE WIND
from WHISTLE DOWN THE WIND

Music by ANDREW LLOYD WEBBER
Lyrics by JIM STEINMAN
Arranged by Phillip Keveren

Moderato con moto

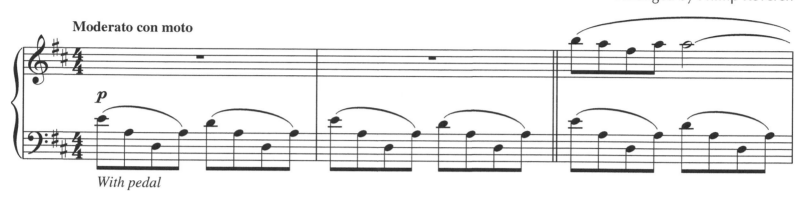

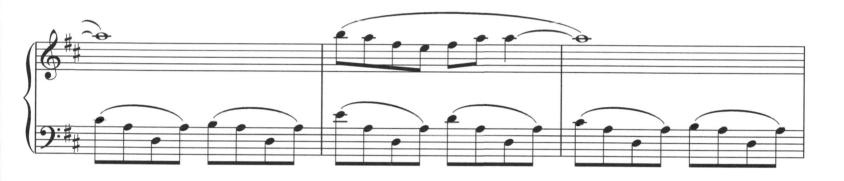

© Copyright 1996, 1998 The Really Useful Group Ltd., Universal - Songs Of PolyGram International, Inc. and Lost Boys Music
This arrangement © Copyright 2003 The Really Useful Group Ltd., Universal - Songs Of PolyGram International, Inc. and Lost Boys Music
All Rights for The Really Useful Group Ltd. in the United States and Canada Administered by Universal - PolyGram International Publishing, Inc.
International Copyright Secured   All Rights Reserved

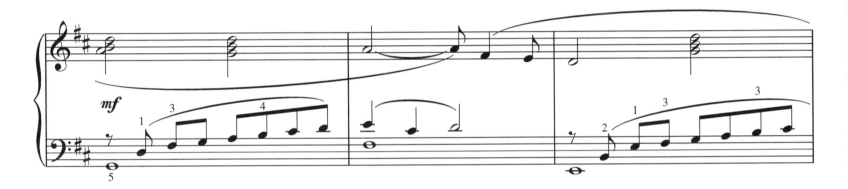

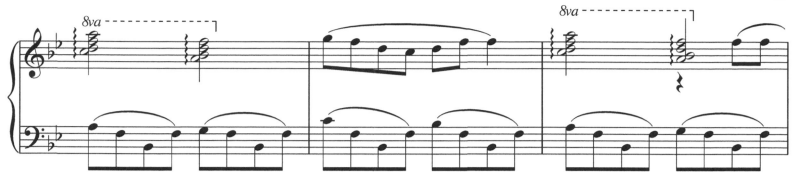

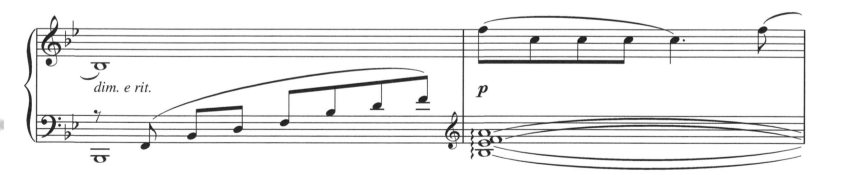

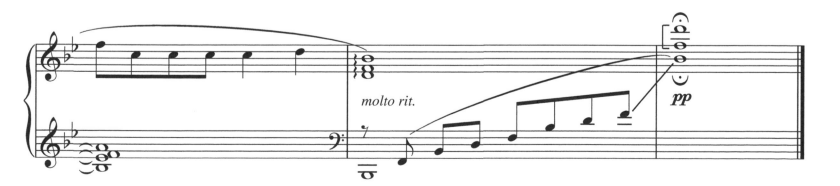

UNEXPECTED SONG
from SONG AND DANCE

Music by ANDREW LLOYD WEBBER
Lyrics by DON BLACK
Arranged by Phillip Keveren

Slowly and gently

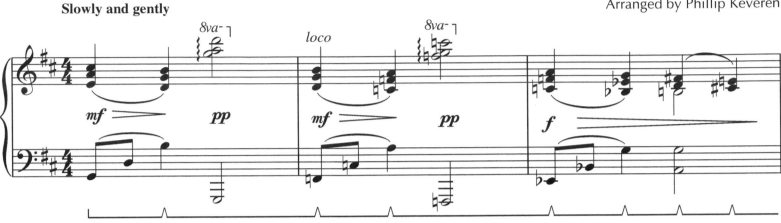

© Copyright 1982 The Really Useful Group Ltd. and Dick James Music Ltd.
This arrangement © Copyright 2003 The Really Useful Group Ltd. and Dick James Music Ltd.
All Rights for the United States and Canada Administered by Universal - PolyGram International Publishing, Inc. and Universal - Songs Of PolyGram International, Inc.
International Copyright Secured   All Rights Reserved

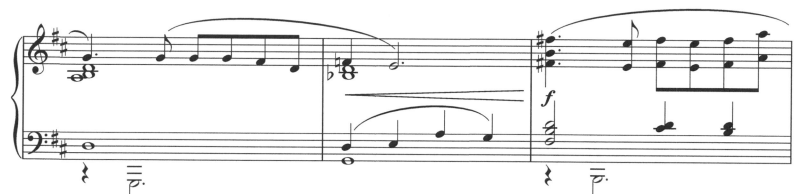

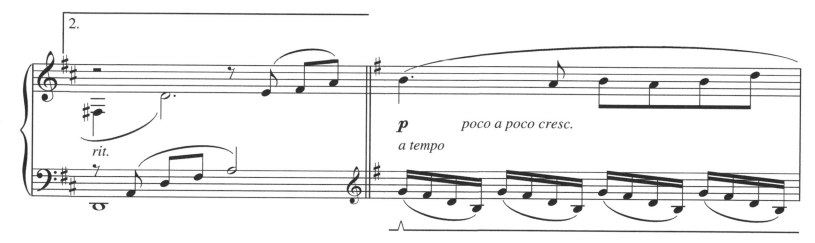

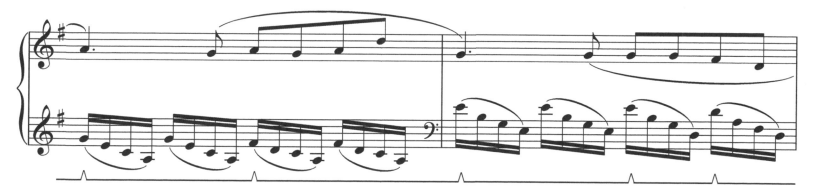

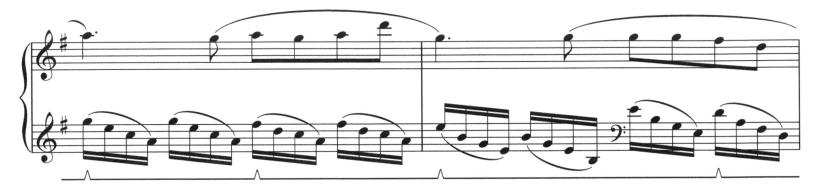

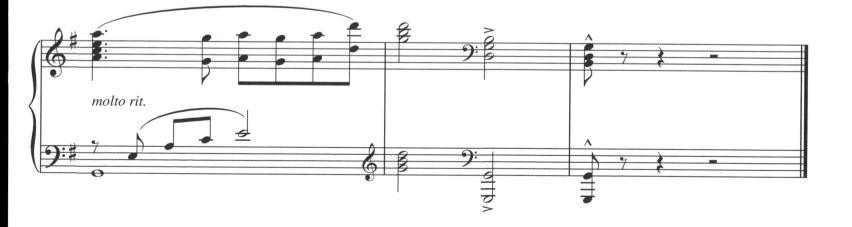

WITH ONE LOOK
from SUNSET BOULEVARD

Music by ANDREW LLOYD WEBBER
Lyrics by DON BLACK and CHRISTOPHER HAMPTON,
with contributions by AMY POWERS
Arranged by Phillip Keveren

Moderately slow, expressively

© Copyright 1993 The Really Useful Group Ltd.
This arrangement © Copyright 2000 The Really Useful Group Ltd.
All Rights for the United States Controlled by Famous Music Corporation
International Copyright Secured   All Rights Reserved

Piu mosso

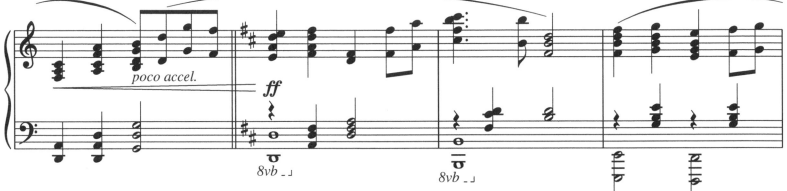

Majestically